LIVING AND WORKING IN
ANCIENT EGYPT

Edited by
Joanne Randolph

Enslow Publishing
101 W. 23rd Street
Suite 240
New York, NY 10011
USA

enslow.com

This edition published in 2018 by:
Enslow Publishing, LLC.
101 W. 23rd Street, Suite 240
New York, NY 10011

Library of Congress Cataloging-in-Publication Date

Names: Randolph, Joanne, editor.
Title: Living and working in Ancient Egypt / edited by Joanne Randolph.
Other titles: Back in time (Enslow Publishing)
Description: New York, NY : Enslow Publishing, 2018. | Series: Back in time | Includes bibliographical references and index.
Identifiers: LCCN 2016057807| ISBN 9780766089662 (6 pack) | ISBN 9780766089679 (library bound book) | ISBN 9780766089655 (pbk. book)
Subjects: LCSH: Egypt—Civilization—To 332 B.C.—Juvenile literature.
Classification: LCC DT61 .L78 2017 | DDC 932/.01—dc23
LC record available at https://lccn.loc.gov/2016057807

Printed in China

To Our Readers: We have done our best to make sure all website addresses in this book were active and appropriate when we went to press. However, the author and the publisher have no control over and assume no liability for the material available on those websites or on any websites they may link to. Any comments or suggestions can be sent by e-mail to customerservice@enslow.com.

Photos Credits: Cover, p. 1 rayints/Shutterstock.com; series logo, jeedlove/Shutterstock.com; back cover, Reinhold Leitner/Shutterstock.com; hourglass on spine, MilaLiu/Shutterstock.com; pp. 4, 17, 26, 30 Ksenia Palimski/Shutterstock.com; p. 5 Peter Hermes Furian/Shutterstock.com; p. 6 Historical Picture Archive/Corbis Historical/Getty Images; pp. 9, 10, 24, 28 DEA/G. Dagli Orti/De Agostini/Getty Images; p. 12 sisqopote/Shutterstock.com; pp. 13, 15, 20, 31 Print Collector/Hulton Archive/Getty Images; p 18 Werner Forman/Universal Images Group/Getty Images; p. 22 Dario Lo Presti/Shutterstock.com; p. 23 Leemage/Corbis Historical/Getty Images; p. 27 Elena Schwartz/EyeEm/Getty Images; p. 32 Universal Images Group/Getty Images; p. 36 Musee du Louvre, Paris, France/De Agostini Picture Library/G. Dagli Orti/Bridgeman Images; pp. 38-39 Heritage Images/Hulton Fine Art Collection/Getty Images; p. 40 DEA/A. Dagli Orti/De Agostini/Getty Images; p. 42 JTB Photo/Universal Images Group/Getty Images.

Article Credits: Peggy Wilgus Wymore, "Growing Up in Another Time," *AppleSeeds*; Ann Jordan, "Egypt: Gift of the Nile," *AppleSeeds*; Joyce Haynes, "School Days," *AppleSeeds*; Joann J. Burch, "Family Fun," *AppleSeeds*; Cyndy Hall, "Pass the Bread," *AppleSeeds*; Kathiann M. Kowalski, "Who Crunched the Numbers in Ancient Egypt?" *AppleSeeds*; Damian Fagan, "All Wrapped Up," *AppleSeeds*; Susan Blair, "Priests and Priestesses: Guardians of the Gods," *AppleSeeds*; Julie Doyle Durway, "Pharaohs: Rulers of Ancient Egypt," *AppleSeeds*; Jane Scherer, "The Boy King," *AppleSeeds*; Jennifer Buchet, "Growing Up a Goddess," *AppleSeeds*; Neil Wright, "Cleopatra's World," *AppleSeeds*; Jane Evans, "Alexandria: Cleopatra's Hometown," *AppleSeeds*.

All articles © by Carus Publishing Company. Reproduced with permission.

All Cricket Media material is copyrighted by Carus Publishing Company, d/b/a Cricket Media, and/or various authors and illustrators. Any commercial use or distribution of material without permission is strictly prohibited. Please visit http://www.cricketmedia.com/info/licensing2 for licensing and http://www.cricketmedia.com for subscriptions.

CONTENTS

CHAPTER 1

GROWING UP IN ANOTHER TIME

R ead these clues. Can you guess what time and place this is? Families spend time together. Kids like acrobatics and music. They like playing with dolls and balls. They like racing and "playing war." Cats and dogs are favorite pets. Sounds like today in America, doesn't it?

But what about this: some babies are given fried mice to chew while teething! Most children don't go to school! Children's heads are often shaved except for one lock of hair worn over the right ear! Kids don't worry about clothes because they don't wear any!

This map shows the Nile River in Egypt. The green areas surrounding the river indicate rich, fertile land. Everything else is desert.

This doesn't sound like your life anymore, does it? Let's travel back about 4,500 years into the past. Go to the northeast corner of Africa along the Nile River. You are now in Egypt when the pyramids were built.

IMAGINE

Suppose you are growing up in that time and place. What is your life like?

Whether you are rich or poor, your house is probably made of mud bricks and is one to three stories tall. Its size depends on your father's job.

Is he the pharaoh? Then your mud brick home would be a palace with many rooms.

Is he a nobleman or a scribe? If so, your large house may have a private courtyard with flowers and a fish pond.

Perhaps you live in one of the great cities, Memphis or Thebes. Your father or mother might be a weaver who makes cloth or might work in a bakery making bread. Then you live in a small house, close to others like yours, with doors opening to a dusty, narrow street.

Probably, though, your father is a farmer. If he is a rich farmer, you may live on a huge farm along the Nile. If he has a small farm, you may live in a tiny town near the fields.

All houses have flat roofs. Because of the hot weather, your family often goes to the roof in the evening to get cool. You might even sleep on the roof. Wherever you live, it is on the sand. Except for a narrow strip of land along the Nile, everyplace is sand. The green land along the river is too precious to build houses on. This is the only place to grow all of the food for the country. Because growing crops is so important, most families farm. At harvest time, everyone helps. Your job may be to tie up the shafts of wheat and put them into bundles.

This illustration recreates frescoes from ancient Egypt showing people spinning thread and weaving cloth. Weaving was one of the jobs you could do in ancient Egypt.

If your father is a farmer, he does not work from June to September. The Nile floods its banks then, and all of the farmland is covered with water. At that time, the pharaoh may order your father to work for him. If not, you have vacation time. Then you might take a boat trip down the Nile with your family. Or you might walk to the next village for a visit, with a donkey carrying your supplies.

Whatever the season, religion is an important part of your life. You probably believe in many gods and wear an amulet, or figure, of one of them on a necklace. Your parents say this protects you from evil and illness.

Childhood is carefree and happy, but it is short. By the time you are a young teenager, you'll be married. So you need training for life and work. You'll get much of this from your parents and some on-the-job training. Like most Egyptian children, you'll be expected to live your life just as your parents have lived theirs.

Right now, though, you're still growing up. You have time to play with your pet *miw* (pronounced "me-you"). Do you know what a miw is? It's a cat!

THE GIFT OF THE NILE

The Nile River was vitally important to ancient Egyptians. It gave them food, water for their crops, and a waterway along which they could transport their goods. A Greek historian once called Egypt "the Gift of the Nile" because the river allowed the nation to grow and thrive. Without the Nile, ancient Egypt probably would not have become the incredibly rich, cultured civilization it was. The lives—and livelihoods—of ancient Egyptians depended on this great river.

It was more than seven thousand years ago that people first settled along the banks of the Nile and began to grow crops in its fertile floodplains. Centuries later, cities developed beside the river. Near the cities, the pharaohs built pyramids to house their tombs and their riches. The Nile begins in the south and flows northward to the Mediterranean Sea.

SCHOOL DAYS

In ancient Egypt, only the very smartest children went to school, where they learned to read and write. Most Egyptians did not ever learn to read and write.

The children who went to school learned to be scribes. Scribes were very important people in ancient Egypt because they were almost the only ones who could read and write. Although records tell us that there were a few female scribes, most were men. Boys entered scribal school when they were quite young and studied hard for about ten to twelve years.

It took years to learn how to write the hundreds of signs called hieroglyphs. Ancient Egyptians used hieroglyphs to write their language. Just think, you only have to learn twenty-six letters!

Scribes also had to know how to write hieratic. This was a kind of shorthand script used for everyday writing.

Students memorized the hieroglyphic signs and practiced writing them on pieces of stone, pottery, or wood. They practiced by copying all kinds of things that had already been written: letters, literature, religious records, and business and government documents. In this way, students learned about more than just their language.

This mural shows Egyptians sailing down the Nile near ancient Thebes. Many Egyptians fished or relied on the Nile to transport their goods.

Scribal students used writing tools somewhat like the parts of a watercolor set you might have. Ink was shaped into round disks, just like our paint sets. But instead of many colors, scribes used only red and black. The cakes of ink were made out of the mineral red ochre and out of black carbon from burnt sticks or pans. Scribes carried small pots of water to mix with the inks. Their brushes, made of reed plants, were held in a small case. The hieroglyph that spells "scribe" contains all of these different parts.

Students often practiced writing on flat pieces of the limestone rock that could be found everywhere in Egypt. Many school texts, or homework, have been found on these flakes of stone. Sometimes a student or a scribe needed to write something very important. Then he wrote on papyrus paper, made from the papyrus plant that grew in the marshes along the Nile.

When a student finished scribe school, he could get a good job in ancient Egypt. He might become a doctor or a priest, the secretary to a noble family, the boss of a group of workers, or have some other job that required the ability to read and write.

The Egyptians wrote as many different kinds of things as we do. They wrote letters home and sent bills for work they had completed. They wrote poetry and stories and put down words of wisdom and advice for their children. They wrote many prayers to their gods.

This painted limestone statue shows a scribe from Pharaoh Cheops' period. Cheops was also called Khufu and was the pharaoh responsible for building the Great Pyramids at Giza.

Parents were happy to pay the high price to send a child to scribal school. Read these words, from a father to his son. They were written about four thousand years ago, to convince the son of the advantages of going to school.

I will make you love writing more than your mother.
I will present its beauties to you.
Now it is greater than any trade.
There is nothing like it in the land.

I have seen the metal worker at his labor…
At the opening of his furnace,
With fingers like claws of a crocodile.
He stinks more than a fish.

The gardener carries a yoke.
He works himself to death.

I'll speak of the fisherman also…
He labors on the river,
Mingling with crocodiles…

So if you know writing, it will go better for you
Than any other profession I've told you about.

A day in the school room is excellent for you.
It is for eternity, its works are (like) stone.

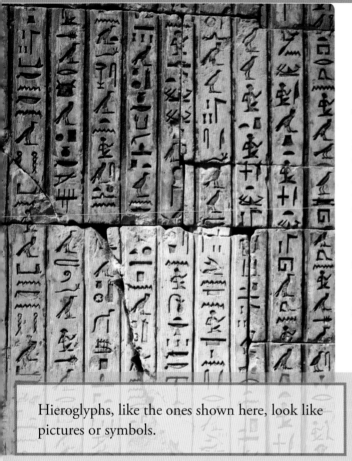

Hieroglyphs, like the ones shown here, look like pictures or symbols.

HIEROGLYPHS

The word *hieroglyph* comes from Greek words meaning "sacred (or holy) carving." The Egyptians called their writing "the words of the gods."

Hieroglyphs were used for about 3,500 years. Then, about 1,300 years ago, Egyptians stopped using them. After that, the meaning of the hieroglyphic signs was lost to the world. No one knew how to read the records and stories and prayers carved on stone sculptures and painted on the walls of tombs. No one could unlock the mysteries of ancient Egyptian history.

However, in about 1822, a French scholar, Jean-Francois Champollion, figured out how to decode hieroglyphs. He worked with the writing on the Rosetta Stone, a stone tablet containing the same message in three different kinds of writing—ancient Greek (which Champollion could read), a kind of hieratic script, and hieroglyphs.

TOYS AND GAMES

Imagine that you are a child of ancient Egypt with nothing to do one afternoon. Suddenly, a friend suggests tug of war, arm wrestling, or a board game. In ancient Egypt? "Yes," says Egyptologist Jennifer Wegner. "Lots of games played by children today are similar to what Egyptian children played thousands of years ago."

This senet board was found in the tomb of Tutankhamun, or "King Tut," who ruled Egypt in the 1300s BCE.

On the walls of Egyptian tombs are pictures of children playing games—games like leap frog and "ring around the rosy." Board games have also been found in tombs and graves. Senet was a board game a little like checkers, chess, and backgammon. Senet was so popular that four game boards were found in King Tut's tomb!

Favorite toys included colorful leather or clay balls, spinning tops, wooden pull-along animals with movable parts, and dolls with string or bead hair. Toys were made from leather, clay, wood, ivory, and dried mud.

FAMILY FUN

Ancient Egyptians loved children, and families had fun together. A favorite outing was to go fishing and hunting in the marshes. These are wet grassy areas along the river or in the delta. (The delta is the place in northern Egypt where the Nile River fans out into many smaller waterways.) The whole family would climb into a boat made from reeds and sail through the marshes.

Children caught fish with spears or nets and picked lotus blossoms. Sometimes the family hunted wild birds with throwing sticks. They picked up the stunned birds that fell from the sky. At home, they put them in a bird house to eat later.

Pharaoh Akhenaten liked having his family around him all the time. When he and his queen, Nefertiti, visited temples or took walks, their daughters were often with them. In the palace, the daughters were usually at their parents' side, even during receptions for important foreign visitors. When the pharaoh went on an inspection tour of his country, he brought his family along.

Egypt's many festivals were a special time for families. There were festivals for the beginning of spring, the harvest, and the flooding of the Nile River. There were festivals for the birth, death, or crowning of a pharaoh.

At festival time, tents and food stalls were set up. People feasted on watermelons, grapes, pomegranates, figs, and little loaves of bread. Sometimes drummers in feathered costumes came from the lands far south of the desert. Bands of young girls played the lute, harp, or flute and women shook the sistrum (a sacred rattle).

This wall painting from the tomb of Nebamun, dating to 1350 BCE, shows an ancient Egyptian banquet.

PASS THE BREAD, PLEASE

What did children eat in ancient Egypt? Did their parents make them finish their vegetables before dessert? Was there any candy? Did kids have peanut butter and jelly sandwiches four thousand years ago?

No one knows for sure if kids in ancient Egypt had to eat all their vegetables. But there are clues in the ruins of tombs and old houses that answer a lot of other questions. Families in ancient

Egypt grew their own food. They planted beans, lentils, onions, leeks, cucumbers, and other crops. Farmers often took heads of "sacred lettuce" to temples to thank the gods for a good harvest.

Fruit trees were everywhere. Children picked their own dates, figs, and pomegranates for afternoon snacks.

The world's first beekeepers were Egyptians. Hives were kept in large pottery jars. Fearless beekeepers simply brushed the bees aside to collect their honeycombs. The honey was stored in covered containers. Children must have enjoyed dipping their fingers in these bowls for a sweet treat.

Perhaps they put honey on their bread, too. In ancient Egypt, children ate bread at every meal. In fact, bread was ancient Egypt's main food. There were hundreds of kinds of bread, in many different shapes and sizes. Some recipes used fruits, garlic, or nuts to flavor the loaves. Eating bread caused some problems, though. Bits of desert sand and stones often got into the dough. Scientists have discovered that most Egyptian mummies have worn and missing teeth. They believe the Egyptians wore their teeth down while chewing on their bread.

So what did ancient Egyptian children eat instead of peanut butter and jelly sandwiches? It's a simple recipe, but probably not one you'll want to try at home. Children cut thick slabs of bread, spread garlic on top, and then piled on raw onions. Yummy...?

Maybe that's why they chewed mint leaves to sweeten their breath!

CHAPTER 2

WORKING IN ANCIENT EGYPT

D o you like math? Maybe you would have been a good surveyor or accountant in ancient Egypt. Or maybe you wanted to help the dead find their way to the afterlife as one of the many people involved in making mummies. Perhaps you found your calling in serving the gods as a priest or priestess. Learn about the different ways ancient Egyptians made a living.

BY THE NUMBERS

In ancient Egypt, not everybody could do math. Most Egyptian "number crunchers" worked for the government performing different jobs. For example, some mathematicians worked as surveyors and measured land. After the Nile's floods each year, surveyors used math to re-measure farmers' fields. Taxes were based partly on the size of a farmer's field, so the government needed to know exactly how large the fields were.

Some Egyptian math whizzes worked as accountants. They tracked how much grain farmers grew, and they kept records of what other workers produced. From this, they determined people's wages, which were often paid with bread or beer.

This wall painting from the tomb of Menna shows two surveyors measuring the wheat before it is cut.

Of course, math also made it possible for ancient Egyptians to build. Everything from palaces to pyramids depended on math.

To prepare themselves for mathematical work, boys worked through number problems at school. One problem might have asked how to divide seven hundred loaves of bread, in certain shares, among four people. Another problem might have asked students to figure out how many bricks a building project needed.

Like us, Egyptians counted by ones, tens, hundreds, and so on. Addition and subtraction were fairly simple. To multiply, Egyptians simply doubled numbers until they could add up the answer. For example, to figure 13 x 11, they first doubled 11 to get 22. Doubling 22 gave them 44, or 4 x 11. And doubling 44 gave them 88, or 8 x 11. Then they added 88 (8 x 11) to 44 (4 x 11) and 11 (1 x 11) to get 143 (8 + 4 + 1 = 13).

Division worked in reverse by repeatedly dividing numbers in half. And Egyptians wrote fractions as the sum of other fractions. For example, two-fifths would be one-third plus one-fifteenth. Are you confused yet?

An ancient Egyptian text called math "the knowledge of all secrets." Maybe you feel that way today when you ace a math quiz!

ALL WRAPPED UP

Ancient Egyptians believed that after a person died, he or she lived on in spiritual form for eternity. To help the spirit reconnect with the body in the afterlife, the body had to be preserved. Mummification was a way to prepare the body for the spirit's return. You probably know that mummies are preserved dead bodies wrapped in strips of cloth. But you might not know how much work and how many different people were involved in making mummies.

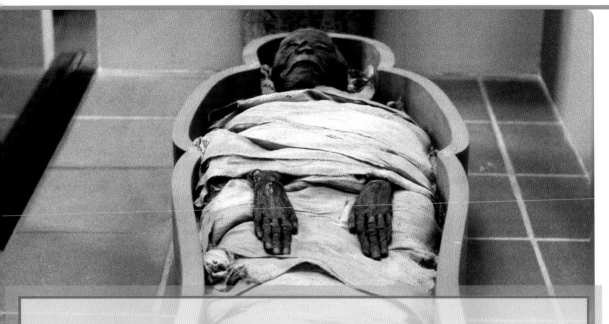

This is an ancient Egyptian mummy in wrappings. It is held in the Vatican Museum in Italy.

The three main processes in mummifying a body were removing the internal organs, drying the body, and protecting the remains. It took about seventy days to make a mummy, with many different people doing different jobs. Let's take a step-by-step look at making a mummy and find out who was involved in the work.

STEP 1. Someone died. If the dead person was a pharaoh, a special burial chamber—perhaps inside a pyramid—had been built while he or she was alive. At first, only pharaohs were mummified. Gradually, members of royal families and wealthy Egyptians could afford the expensive process. But soon mummification was available for all—expensive mummification if you were rich or inexpensive if you were poor.

STEP 2. Embalmers did the main work of making mummies. Some embalmers worked in special buildings; others worked in tents. After washing the body, the embalmer placed it onto a wooden table. Then he made a long cut on the left side of the body, below the ribs. Through this cut, he removed the liver, lungs, stomach, and intestines. (These were mummified separately.) He used a metal hook to pull the brain out through the nose. The heart was usually left in the body. During this process, priests chanted prayers to protect the mummy.

STEP 3. The embalmers and their assistants covered the body with natron, a saltlike chemical collected by natron gatherers along lakeshores. Natron dried the body and prevented bacteria from decaying the body. It could take as long as forty days for the body to dry completely

STEP 4. Once the body was dried, it was cleaned and coated with oils, resins, and perfumes to purify it. Sometimes sawdust or linen pads were put inside the body to fill out the shape. Then the embalmer sewed up the cut and placed jewelry and amulets on the body. (Amulets protected against evil.) Some members of the royal family even had gold caps put onto their fingers and toes.

STEP 5. Using strips of linen, the embalmers wrapped the fingers, toes, arms, and legs individually. Often the arms were folded across the chest. More layers of linen were wrapped around the body. The embalmer painted a sticky resin between the layers as a waterproof layer to protect the mummy. A scribe wrote the dead person's name on one of the bindings. There might be hundreds of yards of linen covering the body. The wrapping process took about fifteen days.

STEP 6. In some cases, a mask was placed over the head. If the dead person was a pharaoh, the mask might be made of gold. The mask was wrapped, then a final cloth covered the entire mummy.

STEP 7. The mummy was placed into a sarcophagus, or coffin.

Sometimes several coffins were nested inside each other, especially if the person was very important or wealthy. The scrolls were placed in the coffin with the mummy to help him or her in the afterlife.

STEP 8. The coffin was brought to the person's home. There, the funeral procession began as family and friends took the coffin to the tomb where the funeral took place. The funeral procession included family, friends, servants, and sometimes professional mourners who cried for the dead.

OTHER PEOPLE WHO HAD A PART IN MUMMY MAKING

Though embalmers did much of the work in making mummies, people from other trades had important parts to play as well. Potters made vases called canopic jars, named after the god Canopus. The embalmer placed the mummified organs into four jars. Each jar was decorated with images of a god and prayers were written on the outside to protect the contents.

Herbalists gathered and made oils, perfumes, resins, and spices from plants

Canopic jars were used to preserve organs of a person being mummified.

growing along the Nile River. The embalmers used some of these substances to clean, dry, and perfume the body, and used others to preserve and wrap the skin. Jewelers made the amulets, necklaces, bracelets, and rings that were placed on the mummy.

Farmers grew and harvested flax plants for their long, strong fibers. Weavers wove these fibers into linen cloth, which was made into rolls of bandages and other cloths. Some linen was also soaked in oils and resins and placed inside the body. Papermakers collected wild reeds, or papyrus, growing along the river and made paperlike scrolls. Scribes wrote spells from the *Book of the Dead* onto these scrolls. The *Book of the Dead* was sort of a guidebook on how to navigate the afterlife. It was intended to help the spirit find its way safely. Artists made portrait masks and painted the coffin with images and hieroglyphics and sculptors and carpenters made coffins as well as artifacts and furniture.

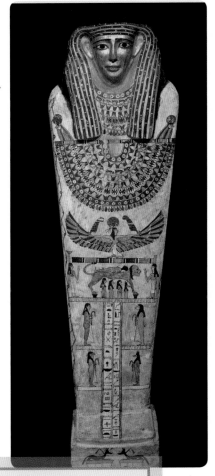

PRIESTS AND PRIESTESSES

In ancient Egypt, religion did not exist separately from everyday life. With as many as two thousand gods and goddesses, Egyptian religion touched every aspect of life. Some gods and goddesses were worshipped throughout the

This is the painted wooden sarcophagus of Chenptah (30 BCE–295 CE), which is displayed in the Louvre Museum in Paris, France.

country; others were worshipped locally. All gods had "jobs," such as ensuring good harvests or protecting people from dangers.

All those gods and goddesses needed daily care and offerings in order to fulfill their expected roles. Egyptians believed that the goddess Maat kept order in the heavens, for example. If she were not satisfied with special ceremonies and offerings, Egyptians feared that chaos would result.

The Egyptian god Horus, often shown with the head of a falcon, was in charge of the sky, moon, and sun.

Each god and goddess had a temple dedicated to him or her. The people in charge of taking care of the gods and their temples were priests and priestesses.

A priest had many duties. Each day before entering the temple, he took a cleansing bath in a sacred pool. After his bath, the priest shaved his face, head, and eyebrows. He cut his fingernails and toenails. Then he put on a clean white linen robe and sandals made of papyrus. Now he was considered pure and ready to enter the temple.

As he moved toward the center of the temple, musicians in the outer area sang a morning song. The priest then broke the seal on the sanctuary, which housed the shrine of the god. Then he lit a torch to wake the god, said his prayers, and burned incense.

The god might be in the form of a live animal, a bird, or a statue made of solid gold. A statue was believed to hold the god's *ka*, or spirit. After washing the statue and covering it with fresh linen and perfumed oil, the priest's morning duties were complete.

Throughout the day, farmers and villagers brought offerings to the god. Because the farmers and villagers were not allowed to enter the temple, the priest took these offerings into the sanctuary to present to the god. After a certain amount of time had passed, the priests believed that the gods were full. Then the priests took the food for themselves. In addition to the priest's temple duties, he planned and organized festivals to honor the god.

At sunset, the priest backed away from the god, sweeping away his footprints as he went. Then he resealed the shrine for the night. Taking care of the gods was a very important job. Priests in ancient Egypt held positions of great privilege and honor.

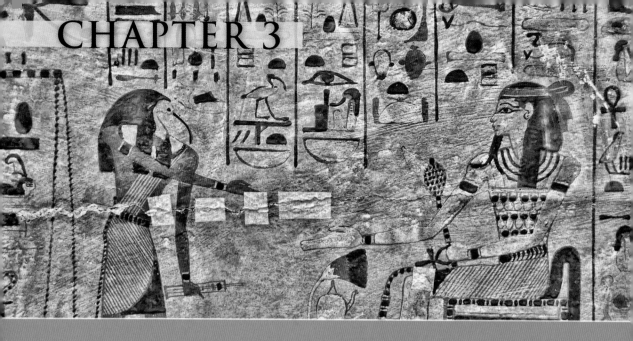

CHAPTER 3

WHO BUILT THE PYRAMIDS?

More than 4,500 years ago, ancient Egyptians first stacked rectangular blocks of stone to build a pyramid. Stepping toward the sky like a 200-foot-tall (61-meter-tall) cake, this pyramid was built to house the body of Pharaoh Djoser for eternity. Around 130 years later, workers began constructing the towering 482-foot-tall (147-meter-tall) "Great Pyramid" for Pharaoh Khufu.

A pyramid began with a command from the pharaoh, who probably began planning his tomb as soon as he became ruler. The pharaoh's high priest chose the site for the pyramid. By studying the stars and making careful calculations, the priest could be sure the four corners of the pyramid would face exactly north, south, east,

More than 2.3 million blocks of limestone and granite were used to construct the pyramid. The total estimated weight of the Great Pyramid is 6.5 million tons (5.9 million metric tons).

and west. The priest made offerings and prayers to the gods at each of these corners. All pyramids were built on the west bank of the Nile. (Egyptians believed that the spirits went to the west bank, to the "heavenly realm," every night.

The pharaoh's chief minister, or official, worked with architects to design the pyramid. Together they planned the location of the king's secret underground burial chamber and other important parts of the pyramid. The minister issued work orders, and scribes wrote out lists of materials.

It Takes a Village to Build a Temple

It took many people doing different jobs to build a pyramid. Tens of thousands of laborers—men and maybe some women—led by architects, engineers, overseers, and other experts did the actual building. During the annual flooding of the Nile, when farmers could not work in their flooded fields, they often worked on the pyramid instead.

To prepare the site, workers leveled the ground on which the foundation would rest. Rock haulers carried small rocks away, and water carriers brought cool relief. At the pyramid site, stonecutters dug rock and cut and shaped it into massive stone blocks. At quarries far upriver, stonecutters cut limestone to make a bright white outer covering for the pyramid. The stones were loaded onto riverboats and transported downriver to the pyramid site.

This is the burial chamber of the pyramid dedicated to the pharaoh Unas in ancient Memphis. There are stars carved into the ceiling and religious writings, called the "Pyramid Texts," on the walls.

At the site, groups of men hauled the stones into place. They constructed a burial chamber for the pharaoh's coffin. They built the rest of the pyramid around that chamber which lay deep inside the structure. Using rocks and mud, workers built ramps to drag the stones higher up the pyramid. Stonemasons carefully carved the blocks so they fit tightly together. When the outer limestone layer was put on, other workers polished the blocks with sand, brought in by the basketful, so that the pyramid sparkled in the sunshine. Finally, a pyramid-shaped capstone was placed on top and covered with gold.

Villages sprang up near the pyramid's construction, housing potters, brick makers, and toolmakers, among others. Doctors tended to the laborers' sprains and broken bones. There were weavers of cloth, bakers of bread, brewers of ale, and cooks. And there were dozens— perhaps hundreds—of scribes, keeping records of everything. The pharaoh's tomb was a work of art for the entire country; everybody had a hand in it. After all, it was a temple to last for eternity and took ages of intense labor to build.

DID SLAVES BUILD THE PYRAMIDS?

Egyptian slaves were enemies captured from foreign countries. Bought and sold like property, they were considered the least important people in Egyptian society. With no rights, they were often badly treated and given the worst jobs.

For many years, historians believed that slaves were the laborers who built the pyramids. But why would a pharaoh use slaves to build his eternal home? In fact, they didn't. Historians have recently discovered that most pyramid laborers were free citizens, proud to work for their pharaoh.

CHAPTER 4

RULERS OF EGYPT

For nearly three thousand years, pharaohs ruled ancient Egypt. An absolute ruler, the pharaoh was king to the Egyptian people. They believed that he—or she—was a god in human form and of Egypt itself. In return for protection and guidance, the people gave the pharaoh complete obedience. An Egyptian nobleman once said about his pharaoh, "He gives everyone safety. He is like a father and mother to all people. No one can equal Pharaoh."

In general, the job of pharaoh was inherited, passed down from one family member to another (usually from a father to a son). Although there was no law against women pharaohs, there were only four who ruled Egypt during the ancient period.

The pharaoh lived in great luxury, surrounded by fine works of art, with hundreds of servants at his command. His main residence was at one of the big cities such as Thebes or Memphis, in a grand palace as large as a small city. Although the pharaoh lived a life of splendor, he was not free to do as he chose. Instead, his days were scheduled according to tradition. His time was filled with ceremonies, dedications, and many other tasks.

This statue of Ramses II stands at Luxor, Egypt. Ramses II was the pharaoh from 1279 to 1213 BCE.

Every day, the pharaoh made decisions that affected the lives of Egyptian citizens. He advised his officials about economic and social issues. He made laws. He monitored the grain harvest. As supreme religious leader, the pharaoh built and dedicated new temples and supervised religious rituals. As commander of the military, he reviewed the troops and consulted with his officers. During wartime, the pharaoh sometimes led his army into battle and made decisions about strategy. As owner of all Egyptian land, he was expected to protect it from invasion and war.

Just as a parent is responsible for his or her child, the pharaoh was responsible for his people: their health and happiness, their harvests, their success in warfare, and even their weather. Of course, the pharaoh could not really control all of these things, but his many

The tomb of King Tutankhamun was found in 1922 and was filled with many artifacts. The period during which King Tut ruled was called the New Kingdom.

duties symbolized his enormous power in the eyes of his people. From the annual flooding of the Nile to a victory in battle, every event in ancient Egypt was identified with the power of the pharaoh.

THE BOY KING

Ruler of all Egypt, believed to be a god, Pharaoh Tutankhamun (tu-tang-KAHM-un) wore a tall crown with a figure of a cobra in the front. A bull's tail on his belt showed his strength. He wore a false beard as a His word was law.

Tutankhamun—sometimes called King Tut—became pharaoh when the pharaoh before him died. He was just nine years old! Because he was so young, advisors helped him rule and held great power. But young Tutankhamun was the king.

When he died nine years later, Tutankhamun was only eighteen years old. Egyptologists suspect that the young pharaoh may have been murdered. We don't know the truth. But in his death, he has told us a great deal about his life.

In 1922, Tutankhamun's tomb was uncovered by Egyptologists. They found in the tomb many objects that told them about the life of the young pharaoh. There were golden statues and cases of jewels. There were models of boats to carry the pharaoh on the Nile and models of servants to help him.

There also were many things from Tutankhamun's childhood: small gloves that he probably wore as a child, brightly colored balls, a wooden cat with a jaw that moved and a tail that wagged. We know that he liked to play games like senet because four senet boards were buried with him. We also know that he liked to hunt because bows and arrows were buried with him.

Tutankhamun lived and died more than 3,300 years ago. We can only wonder what it would be like to rule all of Egypt as a boy king, only nine years old.

GROWING UP AS A GODDESS

Born in 69 BCE, Cleopatra was no ordinary princess. She was born a living goddess!

Cleopatra grew up in immense luxury. She lived in a marble palace in Alexandria, along the shores of the Mediterranean Sea. Even as a child, she wore precious jewels and clothes of the softest silk. She did not lack any necessities or comforts. Her private rooms overlooked the towering Lighthouse, one of the wonders of the world. She even had her own set of servants!

Servants did everything for Princess Thea (ancient Greek for "goddess")—everything from bathing her in honey-scented horse's milk to putting on her jewel-encrusted wigs. They picked up all her toys and even taste-tested her meals for poison. On hot days, they walked behind her, fanning her with giant ostrich feathers. And if she didn't feel like walking, she was carried on a golden couch.

Yet for all her wealth and power, young Cleopatra was just like you in many ways. For instance, she went to school. In fact, she went to school every day, unless it was the festival of Apollo every other month. Unlike you, though, she could use the world's largest library. Cleopatra could study at the Library of Alexandria, which housed hundreds of thousands of handwritten scrolls.

Cleopatra was a smart and eager student. Tutored by private scholars, she studied subjects like math, history, philosophy, biology, astronomy, and music. When Cleopatra read, servants held the heavy scrolls for her. (This made curling up with a good story rather awkward!)

When this gilded goddess wasn't studying her scrolls, traveling around her kingdom, or dining with dignitaries, she relaxed. She enjoyed board games like senet and snake. But she probably didn't play with her brothers and sisters. These royal siblings were always scheming and plotting against one another for the throne.

Instead, Cleopatra hung out with her "foster siblings." These were children from wealthy families who lived with her. The palace grounds were their playground. They raced through tropical gardens, danced over handcrafted mosaic floors, and played tag within the private zoo.

That's right, Cleopatra had her own zoo. Not only did this princess have cats for pets—a must-have for any Egyptian child—she also had antelopes, lions, monkeys, and cheetahs in her personal cages.

Almost all pharaohs—rulers of Egypt—were men. But when Cleopatra's father died, Cleopatra and her younger brother inherited the throne. In those days, royal Egyptians often married their brother or sister to keep the bloodlines pure. Historians say that at the age of eighteen, Cleopatra married her brother. One ceremony was Greek and the other Egyptian. Legend says that Cleopatra dressed as the goddess Isis.

CLEOPATRA'S WORLD

So now you've learned what it was like to grow up for Cleopatra. However, Cleopatra's story begins in 332 BC, hundreds of years before her birth. A powerful leader, Alexander the Great of Macedon, marched an enormous army of Greeks east to Egypt. He freed the

Cleopatra was the last active pharaoh before the Roman Empire took over Egypt.

Egyptian people from the Parthians, a group who controlled them. And he built a city on the Nile, which he named Alexandria. When Alexander died, a Greek general named Ptolemy became king of Egypt.

The great power around the Mediterranean was not Egypt, however. It was Rome. In about 750 BCE, a band of homeless farmers had founded a little town, which grew into a powerful city. By 140 BCE, Rome controlled all of Italy and most of the countries around the Mediterranean Sea. But Rome did not control Egypt.

In 100 BCE, a man named Julius Caesar was born in Rome. Caesar grew up in a time of civil wars, when political thugs seized power by murder. Caesar, a great general, demanded extra power after victories in war. The Roman Senate refused his demand. So Caesar started another civil war by invading Rome and murdering his rivals.

Thirty years after Caesar's birth, Cleopatra was born in Egypt in the year 69 BCE. Her family's history is also filled with murders and takeovers and exiles. With her brother, she became ruler in the year 51 BCE, when her father died. But two years later, her brother chased her out of Alexandria. Cleopatra was not defeated, though. Already unstoppable at twenty-one years of age, she raised an army to fight against her brother.

Then Cleopatra asked the powerful Roman general to help her regain her throne from her brother. Charmed by Cleopatra, Caesar aided the young queen. Then he stayed in Egypt for another year. After Caesar returned to Rome in the year 46 BCE, Cleopatra followed. She brought with her their baby, named Caesarion. Two years later, Caesar was killed in Rome. Men who felt that Caesar had betrayed Rome assassinated him. Cleopatra fled to Egypt with the baby.

Soon Roman leaders who wanted to take over after Caesar were at war with one another. After a great battle, two leaders—Mark Antony and Octavian—agreed to rule together. Octavian stayed in Rome. Antony's task was to conquer Parthia.

This painting shows the meeting between Julius Caesar and Cleopatra. It was painted in 1774 by Giovanni Domenico Tiepolo.

Pretty soon, however, Mark Antony had run out of resources in the East. By then, Cleopatra was the wealthiest person in the world. But she knew that Rome was still more powerful. To protect her country, Cleopatra offered Antony her army and navy in exchange for an alliance with Rome.

Cleopatra charmed Antony as she had Caesar. Together they had three children. Antony also gave her some territories that Rome had conquered from Egypt. This angered the Romans. Finally, Octavian declared war on Antony, his former ally. Octavian met Mark Antony and Cleopatra's armies in battle at Actium in the year

31 BCE. The Roman forces under Octavian won, and Antony and Cleopatra retreated to Egypt. Overpowered and humiliated, they both committed suicide.

In the end, Cleopatra had held onto her country against Rome and the rest of the world for twenty years. When she died, Octavian seized Egypt for Rome.

Cleopatra had lived her incredible life in a world dominated by Rome. Preserving Egypt took intelligence and courage. She managed a navy and an army, controlled a vast wealth, and changed politics in Rome. In the end, however, she was doomed. Rome was already larger than any one enemy could handle.

This painting by Giovanni Domenico Tiepolo shows the meeting between Antony and Cleopatra.

ALEXANDRIA: CLEOPATRA'S HOMETOWN

Even in ancient times, there were tourists, and so there were guidebooks for travelers. Some of the ancient guidebooks listed "seven wonders of the world." Two of them were in Egypt: the Great Pyramid of Giza and the Pharos, or Lighthouse, of Alexandria.

When Alexander the Great conquered Egypt, he decided he needed a new capital. To promote trade, he built a port that would become the largest and busiest harbor in the ancient world. By Cleopatra's time, only Rome was bigger than Alexandria.

The harbor of Alexandria linked the Mediterranean Sea with the Nile River, through Lake Mareotis. Canals allowed boats to travel between the lake and the sea. They carried grain, fruits, and vegetables from the farms of Egypt to the city and the harbor.

Helping to guide the boats into the harbor was one of the seven wonders of the ancient world—the Pharos, or Lighthouse. The stone Pharos was 440 feet (134 meters) high. The Lighthouse keepers kept a smoky fire burning during the day and a bright fire at night. This helped sailors make their way safely into Alexandria.

Cleopatra's palace was near the harbor. It was a huge building and certainly contained many dining rooms, gardens, and bedrooms. There also were rooms for her bodyguard and staff, the people she needed for running her empire.

Today, archaeologists are uncovering the ancient city of Alexandria. They have found statues that probably came from the Temple of Isis in the palace. The goddess Isis became important in Alexandria, since she watched over sailors. There were several

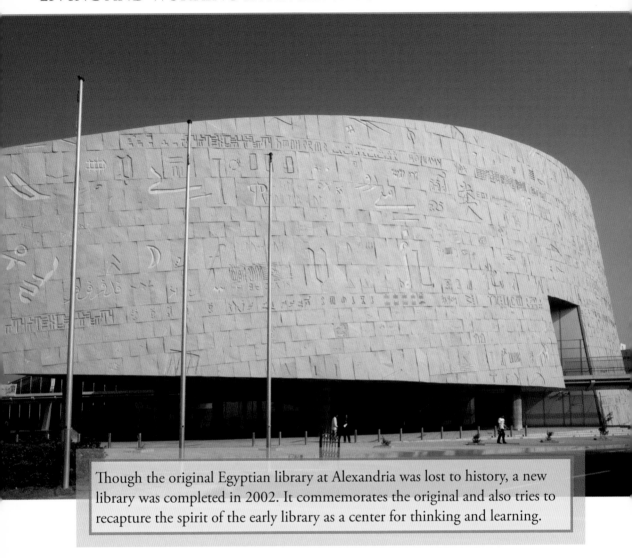

Though the original Egyptian library at Alexandria was lost to history, a new library was completed in 2002. It commemorates the original and also tries to recapture the spirit of the early library as a center for thinking and learning.

temples to Isis in the city, as well as a temple to her husband Serapis. Serapis watched over the crops of Egypt, making the land fertile.

One of the most important buildings in Alexandria was the Library. By the time Cleopatra came to the throne, it may have held more than four hundred thousand scrolls. In the ancient world, it was the largest library ever built.

The Library was part of the Museum. This large building had rooms for research and lectures. There were bedrooms for visiting scholars. Cleopatra paid fifty men to live there to teach and do research. They also tutored the princes and princesses. In a way, it was the first university.

But the city contained more than the royal buildings. There were houses, markets, law courts, a theater, a racecourse, and temples to the important gods. We know that many people went to live there. There were Nubians (from farther south in Africa), Nabateans (from the Middle East), Jews, Greeks, Phoenicians (from an area on the coast of modern Lebanon), and Arabs. Long before Cleopatra's time, a writer exclaimed that this was a city where "every wonder is displayed for all eyes to see."

CHRONOLOGY

c. 5000 BCE Farming comes to the Nile Valley.

c. 3500–3000 BCE The pre-dynastic period, leading to the unification of Egypt.

c. 2650 BCE The beginning of the Old Kingdom.

c. 2575–2465 BCE The Great Pyramids of Giza are built.

c. 2150 BCE The fall of the Old Kingdom leads to the First Intermediate period.

2074 BCE The Middle Kingdom begins; Egypt is united and powerful again.

1759 BCE The fall of the Middle Kingdom leads to the Second Intermediate period, and the occupation of northern Egypt by the Hyksos.

1539 BCE The reunification of Egypt and the expulsion of the Hyksos begin the New Kingdom, a period when Egypt became a leading power in the Middle East.

1344–1336 BCE The pharaoh Akhenaten carries out a short-lived religious reformation.

1336–1327 BCE Tutankhamen reigns.

1279–1213 BCE The reign of Ramses II brings Egypt to the height of its power.

c. 1150 BCE onwards The New Kingdom falls into decline.

728 BCE Egypt is conquered by Nubian kings.

656 BCE Egypt is occupied by the Assyrians.

639 BCE The Egyptians expel the Assyrians and begin a period of revival.

525 BCE Egypt is conquered by the Persians.

332 BCE Egypt is conquered by Alexander the Great.

305 BCE Ptolemy, one of Alexander the Great's generals, founds a Greek-speaking dynasty.

51 BCE Cleopatra, the last queen of independent Egypt in ancient times, reigns.

30 BCE Cleopatra dies and Egypt is annexed by the Roman Empire.

GLOSSARY

amulet A small ornament or piece of jewelry thought to give protection from evil, danger, or illness.

canopic jar A stone or clay jar used to hold the embalmed organs of a dead person in ancient Egypt.

civilization The society, culture, and way of life in a particular area and time.

delta A landform formed by the deposit of materials from a river as it nears its outlet.

embalmer A person who prepares and preserves dead bodies.

festival A day or period of celebration that is often related to a religious holiday or event.

floodplain A low-lying area around a river made up of sediment and prone to flooding.

hieratic Realting to a simpler form of hieroglyphics used by ancient Egyptian priests.

hieroglyphs Symbols used in Egyptian writing to convey words and ideas.

natron A mineral salt found in dry lakebeds.

resin A sticky, water-resistant substance given out by some trees and other plants, such as pine resin.

sacred Connected and dedicated to a religion and God or gods.

sarcophagus A stone coffin used by ancient civilizations.

scribe A person trained to read and write and often to copy documents.

scroll A roll of parchment or paper for writing on.

surveyor A person who studies and measures the land.

tomb A large vault, often underground, used to bury the dead.

FURTHER READING

BOOKS

Amstutz, Lisa J. *Ancient Egypt*. Minneapolis, MN: Essential Library, 2015.

Conklin, Wendy, and Blane Conklin. *You Are There! Ancient Egypt 1336 BC*. New York, NY: Time for Kids Nonfiction Readers, 2016.

Lowery, Zoe, and Susanna Thomas. *Akhenaten and Tutankhamen*. New York, NY: Rosen Publishing Group, 2017.

Nardo, Don. *Cleopatra*. San Diego, CA: ReferencePoint Press, 2016.

Nardo, Don. *Life in Ancient Egypt*. San Diego, CA: ReferencePoint Press, 2014.

WEBSITES

The British Museum
www.ancientegypt.co.uk/menu.html
Visit the British Museum website to explore Egyptian life, religion, pyramids, writing, and more.

DK Find Out!
www.dkfindout.com/us/history/ancient-egypt/
Discover more about ancient Egyptian culture.

National Geographic Kids
www.ngkids.co.uk/history/ten-facts-about-ancient-egypt
Read ten quick facts about ancient Egypt.

INDEX